Essential Guidance Senior Cycle Learner's Record©

Copyright © Classroom Guidance Ltd

Published by Classroom Guidance Ltd

This fourth edition was written by Brian Comerford *BEng HDGE* & Fred Tuite *BA HDGE*

for Classroom Guidance Ltd 2020.

Editor: Jennifer Rope *BA HDAA*

A special thanks to Jean Rodgers, Richard Kean and Joe Duddy for their support and advice.

www.classroomguidance.ie

Table of Contents

Guidance Appointment Worksheet

Before you visit your Guidance Counsellor, complete the Guidance Appointment Worksheet below:

Name: _____ Class: _____ Date: _____

Facts: How I did in the Junior Certificate:

....

Favourite Subjects:

....

Hobbies & Interests:

....

Plans: Where I want to go / what I want to do:

....

Career areas I am interested in:

....

Colleges /courses I am interested in:

....

Apprenticeships / training I would like to do:

....

Actions: What steps I have taken: *Circle*

<u>CAO:</u> Research,   Apply,   Revise,   Finalise

<u>UCAS:</u> Research,   Colleges,   Personal Statement,   Apply,   Test,   Interview,   Decide

<u>PLC</u>: Research,   Apply,   Interview

<u>Work or Training:</u> Research,   CV,   Apply,   Interview

---

Limitations: What hinders me:

Subjects: ....

Points: ....   Money: ....

Geography: ....   Health: ....

Dreams: I would really love to ....

If I had the talent or money I would ....

This may sound crazy but ....

1

My Top Six Courses

Course Name	1st Year Subjects		Benefit To Me
	1		
	2		
	3		
Code	4		
Level	5		
My % Rating:	6		
	7		
	8		

Course Name	1st Year Subjects		Benefit To Me
	1		
	2		
	3		
Code	4		
Level	5		
My % Rating:	6		
	7		
	8		

Course Name	1st Year Subjects		Benefit To Me
	1		
	2		
	3		
Code	4		
Level	5		
My % Rating:	6		
	7		
	8		

Course Name		1st year Subjects	Benefit To Me
	1		
	2		
	3		
Code	4		
Level	5		
My % Rating:	6		
	7		
	8		

Course Name		1st year Subjects	Benefit To Me
	1		
	2		
	3		
Code	4		
Level	5		
My % Rating:	6		
	7		
	8		

Course Name		1st Year Subjects	Benefit To Me
	1		
	2		
	3		
Code	4		
Level	5		
My % Rating:	6		
	7		
	8		

3

5TH YEAR

UNIT 1

My Goal

Whatever you want to be in the long term, name it!

Set your short-term goal:

Let's Get SMART

S	
M	
A	
R	
T	

5

Study Time Table

Fill in your study times and the subjects you will study at each time. By the way, study is what you do *after* your homework!

Period / Time / Day	Monday	Tuesday	Wednesday	Thursday	Friday	Saturday	Sunday
1 _____							
2 _____							
3 _____							
4 _____							
5 _____							

6

Seven Steps To Continuous Self-Motivation

Fill in the seven steps:

1	
2	
3	
4	
5	
6	
7	

Quiz Time

1. What percent of students have clear, written, specific, measurable goals?
   a) 3% ☐
   b) 20% ☐
   c) 10% ☐
   d) 60% ☐

2. If you have a clear goal, how much more of a chance do you have in achieving it?
   a) Twice as likely ☐
   b) Doesn't make a difference ☐
   c) 10 times better chance ☐
   d) Less likely to achieve anything ☐

3. Which one of these is <u>not</u> part of the SMART Goals System?
   a) Timely ☐
   b) Actionable ☐
   c) Meaningful ☐
   d) Specific ☐

4. If you don't try you will be...?
   a) Desperate ☐
   b) Doomed ☐
   c) Disappointed ☐
   d) Delighted ☐

5. How do you eat an elephant?
   a) Liquidise it and drink ☐
   b) One bite at a time ☐
   c) Not possible ☐
   d) With tomato sauce ☐

Your score out of 5:

UNIT 2

The Seven Habits Of Effective Students

What is a habit?

How long do habits take to form?

What types of habits are there?

Habit #1 Be Proactive

Define Proactive:

Your Goal from Unit 1 (page 5)

What are the three parts to being proactive?

1	
2	
3	

Do Not Photocopy Thank You

Do you, in general, make proactive or reactive choices? *Circle*

Reactive   Proactive

Can you turn some reactive statements into proactive ones?

Instead of saying....	Say
I don't have time to study	
Why should I bother with this?	
I'm too tired	
I've never been very good at maths	
What is the meaning of life?	

Habit #2 Begin With The End In Mind

Companies' mission statements quiz.

Company Name	
1	
2	
3	
4	
5	

Do Not Photocopy Thank You

Create a personal mission statement for the next few years. This is what you want to achieve, to be, to become and to fulfil.

Habit #3 Put First Things First

Shade in grid below to represent how much time you spend in each quadrant

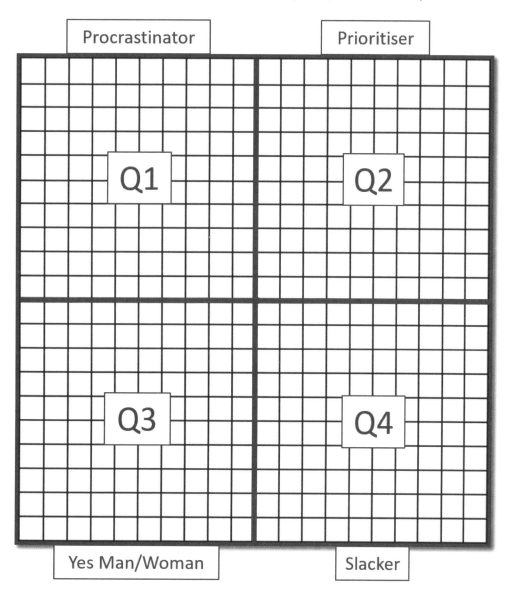

11

Will this allow you to achieve your goals?   *Circle*   **Yes**   **No**

Are there any changes you need to make in your lifestyle?

```



```

Habit #4 Think 'Win-Win'

Write down what you can do to create a 'Win-Win' atmosphere in your school:

```



```

Habit #5 First Listen To Understand

Swap books and rank from **1** (most) to **6** (least) the ways in which your friend listens:

Thinking about what to say next	
Daydreaming	
Thinking about something you need to do later	
Paying absolute attention	
Coming in and out of attention	
Other	

Habit #6 Synergise

Is there a synergy in your class?   *Circle*   **Yes**   **No**

How could you work together better?

```

```

Habit #7 Monthly Review

Why should I review the habits?

```

```

The Marshmallow Challenge

How high was your team's tower? _____

Thinking about the seven habits, what did you learn about yourself by doing this exercise?

```

```

Quiz Time

1. **How long does it take for a habit to form?**
   a) 2 – 10 days ☐
   b) 18 - 40 days ☐
   c) 365 days ☐
   d) 183 days ☐

2. **Reactive people in general**
   a) Plan their lives well ☐
   b) Drink a lot of alcohol ☐
   c) Live lives largely out of control ☐
   d) Are responsible for their own happiness ☐

3. **Proactive people in general**
   a) Let things happen to them ☐
   b) Drink a lot of alcohol ☐
   c) Live lives largely out of control ☐
   d) Are responsible for their own happiness ☐

4. **How much more can geese fly in a "V" formation than alone?**
   a) No more; the same ☐
   b) 71% further ☐
   c) Geese can't fly ☐
   d) 21% further ☐

5. **What is synergy?**
   a) A super free energy from space ☐
   b) Working on your own to gain best results ☐
   c) A computer software package ☐
   d) Working together to create something better ☐

6. **What type of person should you try to be in order to achieve more?**
   a) The Procrastinator ☐
   b) The Yes Man/Woman ☐
   c) The Prioritiser ☐
   d) The Slacker ☐

Your Score out of 6: ____

UNIT 3

Open Days & Career Expos

Use this sheet to get the most from your visit (photocopy as many as you need).

Course: _____ College: _____

What are the main areas studied in this course?

How is the work divided between lectures, tutorials and laboratory work?

Is there a work placement as part of the course? At what stage?

What sort of exams and assessment do you have to do? At what stage?

Do you have to buy any special equipment for this course?

What areas of this course do students have most difficulty with?

Can you do a year / semester abroad with this course?

Are there school subjects that are important for this course?

Where are graduates of this course finding employment?

How is this course different from similar courses in other colleges?

Am I still interested?

15

UNIT 4

Studying: Do It Well

List your results. (QR code for mobile devices links to on-line Learning Style Quiz).

	My Top Learning Styles	How To Apply This Learning Style
1		
2		
3		
4		
5		

Fill in the Forgetting Curve

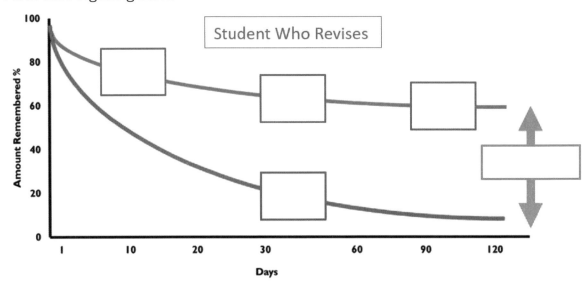

Plan a study session using S.M.A.R.T. Goals

S	
M	
A	
R	
T	

Clever Ways To Study

1	
2	
3	
4	
5	
6	
7	
8	
9	
10	

Reading Well

Write down the three steps to reading well:

1	
2	
3	

Quiz Time

1. Learning styles help you:
   a) Look good when you study ☐
   b) Understand there are often better, more engaging ways to learn ☐
   c) That you must apply one style to all your learning ☐
   d) Have an excuse for not learning ☐

2. If you don't study, what is the difference in % remembered?
   a) 50% ☐
   b) 25% ☐
   c) 90% ☐
   d) No difference ☐

3. What is a good amount of time to study before taking a small break?
   a) One hour ☐
   b) One and a half hours ☐
   c) 40 minutes ☐
   d) 10 minutes ☐

4. As the Leaving Cert approaches, I will need to:
   a) Quit all sports and hobbies ☐
   b) Have a balanced life and don't give up hobbies ☐
   c) Get used to sport drinks ☐
   d) Become good at cramming ☐

5. When note-taking:
   a) Try and condense as much information as possible ☐
   b) Highlight everything ☐
   c) Less is more ☐
   d) Re-write your textbook ☐

6. Past papers are:
   a) Very effective and I should use them ☐
   b) A waste of time and money ☐
   c) Only to be used before the mocks ☐
   d) In the past and I should look to the future ☐

Your Score out of 6: ☐

UNIT 5

Uniqueness & Difference

Careers and people can be categorised into six types. Which types are you? You may be more than one.

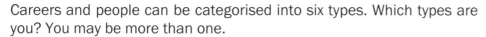

1	Practical people & Manual work	4	Creative people & Artistic work
2	Investigative people & Scientific work	5	Persuasive people & Influencing work
3	Caring people & Social work	6	Organising people & Clerical work

If you've not already done it electronically, give **12 points** to your number one choice, **10 points** to your number two and so on. Your last choice should be given **2 points** (QR code for mobile devices links to this Careers Test on-line).

Ignoring points or salaries, rate your favourite careers:

Description	Code	Score
Electrician	M	
Scientist	U	
Social Worker	S	
Musician	A	
Solicitor	I	
Accountant	C	

Description	Code	Score
Mechanic	M	
Dietitian	U	
Nurse	S	
Hairdresser	A	
Lab Technician	I	
Secretary	C	

Which tasks would you like most?

Description	Code	Score
Fixing things	M	
Investigating things	U	
Helping people	S	
Creating new things	A	
Persuading people	I	
Organising things	C	

Description	Code	Score
Build a wall	M	
Investigate a crime	U	
Listen to someone	S	
Paint a picture	A	
Sell a house	I	
Check accounts	C	

Which tools would you rather use?

Description	Code	Score
Electric drill	M	
Microscope	U	
Social media	S	
Brush & paints	A	
Word	I	
Excel	C	

Which website would you visit first?

Description	Code	Score
How stuff works	M	
NASA Space Centre	U	
Facebook	S	
National Gallery	A	
RTE News	I	
The Economist	C	

Which television shows appeal to you most?

Description	Code	Score
Home improvements	M	
Nature documentaries	U	
Reality T.V.	S	
Arts programmes	A	
Current affairs	I	
Business programmes	C	

Which 'Self Help' book would you choose first?

Description	Code	Score
How to surf	M	
How to program computers	U	
How to do lip reading	S	
How to draw	A	
How to 'Succeed at Sales'	I	
How to do word processing	C	

What do you use your computer for?

Description	Code	Score
Playing games	M	
Doing research	U	
Social media	S	
Photoshop	A	
Sending out your C.V.	I	
Tracking your savings	C	

Which words would describe you best?

Description	Code	Score
Practical	M	
Curious	U	
Helpful	S	
Creative	A	
Enterprising	I	
Orderly	C	

Now, add up all your scores under each letter to get an idea of the type of person you are and the types of careers that may interest you. **Remember:** every job involves an element of all of these categories; so it is important to think out fully what is involved in a career including the elements that are not your favourite or strongest points.

	M Manual Practical	U Understanding Investigative	S Social	A Artistic Creative	I Influencing Persuasive	C Clerical Organisational
Total						
Rank 1-6						

Using your results, suggest three careers/jobs that might suit you:

1	
2	
3	

What Types Of Tasks?

Look at your three suggested careers under the *M U S I A C* headings and detail the different activities involved.

Profession / Type of Task	Doctor	Your choice 1	Your choice 2	Your choice 3 ....
Manual Practical	Stitching a wound			
Understanding Investigative	Knowing the cause and treatment of measles.			
Social	Dealing with a patient and their relatives.			
Influencing Persuasive	Getting someone to stop smoking to avoid having their foot amputated.			
Artistic Creative	Finding ways to cope with a hypochondriac.			
Clerical Organisational	Keeping records of visits and medicines proscribed.			

Remember: however much you are attracted to a career because it suits your type, you will also have to do a lot of tasks that ***don't*** appeal to you that much. Give examples of such tasks from one of your above choices:

Quiz Time

1. Careers and people could be categorised into:
    a) Those with money and those without money ☐
    b) Manual, Artistic, Understanding, Social, Influencing & Clerical ☐
    c) Those who can watch soccer on TV and everyone else ☐
    d) People who have tattoos and people with piercings ☐

2. All jobs:
    a) Have parts to them that are boring or unpleasant ☐
    b) Grind you down till you quit ☐
    c) Are wonderful and fulfilling and give meaning to your life ☐
    d) Are an opportunity to better yourself ☐

3. What job would suit you best with a high Social score?
    a) Accountant ☐
    b) Coal miner ☐
    c) Research scientist ☐
    d) Nurse ☐

4. If you have a high Investigative score what would be your best match?
    a) Football coach ☐
    b) Potter ☐
    c) Research scientist ☐
    d) Salesman ☐

5. What percentage of people dislike what they do?
    a) 10% ☐
    b) 20% ☐
    c) 60% ☐
    d) 90% ☐

Your Score out of :5

UNIT 6

Skills, Qualities & Values

Skills Audit   A skill is something you are good at doing. You have already developed a range of Transferable Skills - skills you have in one area (sport or hobby) you can use in another (work). Employers look for these skills. If you've not already done this electronically, rank your skills in order 1 (being your strongest) to 10 (being your weakest).(QR code for mobile devices links to this Skills Audit on-line).

Critical Problem Solving:	**RANK 1-10**
Critical problem solving refers to your ability to use knowledge, facts, and data to effectively solve problems. This does not mean you need to have an immediate answer, it means you must be able to think on your feet, assess problems and find solutions.	

Critical Thinking Skills:	**RANK 1-10**
Critical thinking skills is the act of analysing facts to understand a problem or topic thoroughly. Critical thinking is the *process* of identifying a problem or issue and developing a solution.	

Creativity Skills:	**RANK 1-10**
Creativity is the ability to think about a task or a problem in a new or different way, or the ability to use your imagination to generate new ideas. Creativity enables you to solve complex problems or find interesting ways to approach tasks. If you are creative, you look at things from a unique perspective.	

People Management Skills:	**RANK 1-10**
People management is the process of training, motivating and directing people in order to optimise productivity and promote growth. Team leaders, managers and department heads use people management skills to oversee work and boost performance every day.	

Coordinating With Others Skills:	**RANK 1-10**
Coordination is an orderly arrangement of group efforts to maintain harmony among individuals and accomplish a common goal.	

Emotional Intelligence (E.Q.): Emotional intelligence is the ability to understand, use, and manage your own emotions in positive ways e.g. to relieve stress, communicate effectively, empathise with others, overcome challenges and defuse conflict.	**RANK 1-10**

Judgement & Decision-Making Skills: Judgment & decision-making skills demonstrate the ability to make considered and effective decisions, come to sensible conclusions, perceive and distinguish relationships, understand situations and form objective opinions.	**RANK 1-10**

Service Orientation Skills: Service orientation skills demonstrate an awareness of and a positive attitude towards customers when responding to their needs and expectations.	**RANK 1-10**

Negotiation Skills: Negotiation skills are qualities that allow two or more parties to reach a compromise. These are often soft skills and include abilities such as communication, persuasion, planning and cooperating. Understanding these skills is the first step to becoming a stronger negotiator.	**RANK 1-10**

Cognitive Flexibility Skills: Cognitive flexibility is the ability to adjust your thinking and habits from old situations to new situations.	**RANK 1-10**

A Skill Not Mentioned: eg art, music, sport. Example from your life:	

24

Qualities Audit

A quality is a particular aspect of your personality / make up and can be useful in certain employment situations, as different employers seek out different qualities in their staff.

If you've not already done this electronically, rank your qualities in order **1** (being your strongest) to **8** (being your weakest). (QR code for mobile devices links to Qualities Audit on-line).

Expressive: I find it easy to communicate. I can get my point across. I am good at explaining things. **Where do you show this?**	**RANK 1-8**

Persistent: I am slow to give up. I bounce back from setbacks. I have grit and determination. **Example from your own experience:**	**RANK 1-8**

Empathic: I feel another person's pain. I can understand what is happening to them and support them. **Example from your own experience:**	**RANK 1-8**

Creative: I can be creative in making something, interpreting something or finding a new solution. I can think 'outside the box'. **Example from your own experience:**	**RANK 1-8**

Intuitive: I have the ability to understand something immediately. I trust my 'gut instinct'. **Example from your life:**	**RANK 1-8**

Enthusiastic: I have an intense desire or passion for something. **Where do you show this?**	**RANK 1-8**

A Good Listener: I take notice of what someone says and respond in the right way. **Example from your life:**	**RANK 1-8**

Persuasive: I am good at persuading someone to do or believe something through reasoning or the use of temptation. **Example from your life:**	**RANK 1-8**

Skills / Qualities Sum-Up

My Top Skills		My Top Qualities	
1		1	
2		2	
3		3	

Do your strengths in your skills and qualities point towards a particular job(s)/career(s)?

26

Values Audit

Our values & beliefs influence the choices we make whether we realise it or not. If you are aware of your values, you can make better choices for your future work. The checklist below will help you discover what area of work you will be happiest in.

If you've not already done it electronically, score each value; 5 (being essential), down to 1 (being unimportant).(QR code for mobile devices linked to this Values Audit on-line).

	Occupational Values	Scoring				
1.	Variety at work	5	4	3	2	1
2.	Experience adventure / excitement	5	4	3	2	1
3.	Travel often	5	4	3	2	1
4.	Work in a fast-paced environment	5	4	3	2	1
Valuing Variety Score						
1.	Be an expert	5	4	3	2	1
2.	Feel respected for your work	5	4	3	2	1
3.	Have power and control	5	4	3	2	1
4.	Well paid	5	4	3	2	1
Valuing Status Score						
1.	Help others	5	4	3	2	1
2.	Have lots of public contact	5	4	3	2	1
3.	Work in a team	5	4	3	2	1
4.	Be active in your community	5	4	3	2	1
Valuing People Score						
1.	Be your own boss	5	4	3	2	1
2.	Set your own hours / have flexibility	5	4	3	2	1
3.	Spend time with family	5	4	3	2	1
4.	Don't need much money to be happy	5	4	3	2	1
Valuing Autonomy Score						
1.	Feel free to suggest solutions and speak your mind	5	4	3	2	1
2.	Opportunities to express your creativity	5	4	3	2	1
3.	Be involved in problem solving	5	4	3	2	1
4.	Have freedom to start projects	5	4	3	2	1
Valuing Creativity Score						
1.	Low risk of being made redundant	5	4	3	2	1
2.	Working according to fixed rules	5	4	3	2	1
3.	Work in a comfortable environment	5	4	3	2	1
4.	A salary that increases slowly each year	5	4	3	2	1
Valuing Security Score						

Using the results from the values audit complete the table below. Write down your values from the highest score to the lowest.

My Values

1st	
2nd	
3rd	
4th	
5th	
6th	

Write a brief paragraph on how compatible your values will be with the career or job you are thinking about for the future. Try to select a job that will help you live your values.

Job I am considering: _____

Is this job compatible with your values?   *Circle*   **Yes**   **No**

Explain your answer:

Quiz Time

1. What is a transferable skill?
   a) When you teach someone how to do something ☐
   b) It's a skill that exists in all countries regardless of religion ☐
   c) Skills you have in one area that you can use in another ☐
   d) A type of currency used on the internet ☐

2. What is a quality?
   a) A quality is a particular aspect of your personality ☐
   b) It's a measure of how tasty something is ☐
   c) A way of saying something is excellent ☐
   d) A stamp on goods to say they passed an inspection ☐

3. What is a value?
   a) A value is something we hold dear; it expresses who we are ☐
   b) What we get on Black Friday ☐
   c) A two for one meal in a café of our choice ☐
   d) A rating on currency ☐

4. When considering a job, which is more important?
   a) Values ☐
   b) Skills ☐
   c) Qualities ☐
   d) All three ☐

5. An average person will change jobs _____ times before they retire.
   a) 11 times ☐
   b) Once ☐
   c) 17 times ☐
   d) Twice ☐

Your Score out of 5:

UNIT 7

Qualifax - A User's Guide

(This class is best done in a computer room if possible.)

What is it?

What can it do for me?

How?

1	
2	
3	
4	

How can I find out more?

1	
2	
3	
4	

UNIT 8

Career Investigation / LCVP Overlap

Choosing A Career

Write down the career you want to investigate. If you don't know, look at the suggestions on page 20 of this book or use the interest assessments in Qualifax, Classroom Guidance or Careersportal to help.

The career I've chosen to investigate is:

Job/career description:

Write down your aim and what you want to achieve from doing this investigation:

Why do you want to achieve it?

Research & Planning

Action Plan

Write in what needs to be done for you to understand everything about the job/career.

Order	Things To Do
1st	Do careers interest test
2nd	Select the carer of your choice to investigate
3rd	Find a company on-line which does that job & research it.
4th	Find someone in that company that can help you learn more about this career
5th	Arrange a meeting with this person & interview them.
6th	Research x1 PLC course & x1 College course that relate to this career.
7th	Interview with your Guidance Counsellor
8th	Rate your performance
9th	Other
10th	Other

Real Life Example

Using the company website, complete a short report on an organisation where the job you are investigating is done.

Company Name	
Mission Statement	
Established	
History	
Product / Service Description	
No. Of People Working There	
No. Of People Doing Your Job	

People - Who Can Help?

List people that could help you find out about the job.

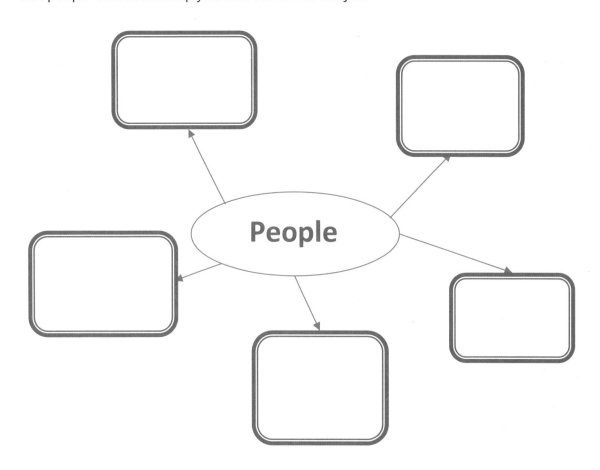

Planning Your Meeting

Choose one person from above:

Why have you chosen this person?

When are you going to make contact to set up an interview or to work shadow?

| Interview | Yes | ☐ | No | ☐ |

| Work Shadow | Yes | ☐ | No | ☐ |

Name	
Company	
Address	
Phone number	
Date Of Meeting		Time	

Alternative Solutions

If the person is unavailable for interview, how else will you find the information you need?

The Interview

Keep a written account of any interviews done:

Person's Name	
Job Title	
Date of interview	
Time of interview	
Place of interview	
Aim of the interview	

35

Interview Questions

Why did you choose this career?

Answer

Do you find the career interesting?

Answer

What training was involved?

Answer

Are you paid well?

Answer

What equipment do you use every day?

Answer

What type of environment do you work in?

Answer

Do you work on your own or with others?

> Answer

What are the key skills and qualities involved in this job?

Skills	Personal Qualities

What are the bad things about the job?

> Answer

What are the good things about the job?

> Answer

Education - Courses

Investigate two courses that allow progression to your area of interest.

<u>Course 1 - Level 6, 7 or 8.</u>

Course Title	
College Name	
Minimum Entry Requirements	
Subjects Taught	1. 2. 3. 4. 5. 6. 7. 8.
No. of Years	
Qualification Earned	
Options For Graduates	

38

Course 2 - Level 5 or PLC

Course Title	
College Name	
Minimum Entry Requirements	
Subjects Taught	1. 2. 3. 4. 5. 6. 7. 8.
No. of Years	
Qualification Earned	
Options For Graduates	

Other route eg. Apprenticeship, Traineeship or 'On-The-Job' Training.

Details:

39

Guidance Counsellor – Interview

Appointment	Date ..../............/............ Time ....

Do you think I am suited to this career? Why?

Answer

What is the future like for this career?

Answer

Will the qualifications that I get from school allow me to start my career?

Answer

Is there a course in college / further education I should consider doing?

Answer

40

Conclusions

Write down your aim(s) again from page 31

Aims

Did you achieve your aim(s)?   Yes [ ]   No [ ]

Why?

What was the most useful piece of research from your investigation?

Why?

List two things you learned about yourself while doing this investigation:

1.	2.

Write down any skills or qualities you now know you have:

Skills	Qualities

Do you still want to do this job/career?　　　Yes ☐　　　No ☐

Why?

Rate Your Performance

Rate your overall performance by circling one of the below descriptions:

Excellent　　　Very Good　　　Good　　　Fair　　　Poor

Why did you rate yourself this way?

Answer

Things I Did Well	
1	
2	
3	

42

Things To Do Better Next Time	
1	
2	
3	

LCVP Marking Scheme

This is what the LCVP marking scheme looks like.

Areas Given Marks	Marks
Title/Word processing/use of headings (or audio communication in clear and confident manner)	0-5
Description of duties involved in the careers area	0-3
Identification of skills and qualities needed	0-5
Identification of qualifications and training needed	0-5
Description of two different pathways to the career	0-4
What was learned by the research/activity about career and oneself	0-8
Evaluation of the career	0-5
Evaluation of undertaking the career investigation	0-5
Total	40

Appendix

Include the following evidence here to **personalise** your investigation:

College Open Day & Prospectus

College Website &/or Company Website

Emails / Letters

Interviews, Surveys & Photos.

Quiz Time

1. When investigating a career, it is a good idea to:
   a) Look at education, work environment & people ☐
   b) Watch a lot of American TV dramas ☐
   c) Not bother as it will be grand, I'm fairly sure about work ☐
   d) Look exclusively on-line as all you need to know is there ☐

2. A Meteorologist's job is to:
   a) Look at and examine meteors ☐
   b) Study and predict the weather ☐
   c) Work for a mobile phone company ☐
   d) To observe the universe and record gravity waves ☐

3. What is a Paediatrician?
   a) A professional that cares for feet ☐
   b) Someone who grows vegetables in green houses ☐
   c) A type of electrician that specialises in computer electronics ☐
   d) A doctor who has special training in medical care for children ☐

4. What is a Barista?
   a) A Spanish barman ☐
   b) A person who defends you in a court of law ☐
   c) A person who is an expert in making coffee ☐
   d) An Italian name for a welder ☐

5. What does an Archivist do?
   a) Restores arches mainly in historical buildings ☐
   b) Builds beehives ☐
   c) Recruits people for the army ☐
   d) Organises archival records and develops classification systems ☐

6. What is a Toxicologist?
   a) Someone who studies the impact of toxic materials on animals ☐
   b) A stamp collector ☐
   c) A person that regulates taxis in a city ☐
   d) Someone who stuffs and preserves dead animals ☐

Your Score out of 6:

44

Do Not Photocopy Thank You

UNIT 9

Jobsearch Practice / LCVP Overlap

Fill in the six steps of how companies hire:

How Companies Hire	
Step 1	
Step 2	
Step 3	
Step 4	
Step 5	
Step 6	

Fill in the five steps you should follow when emailing your CV & Cover Letter:

Emailing CV & Cover Letter	
Step 1	
Step 2	
Step 3	
Step 4	
Step 5	

Application Forms

Write down six good points to remember when filling out an application form:

1	
2	
3	
4	
5	
6	

Practice Application Form

Application for Employment

Our policy is to provide equal employment opportunity to all qualified persons without regard to race, creed, religious belief, gender, age, ancestry, physical or mental disability.

First Name _____ Last Name _____

Address _____

Telephone _____

Position applied for _____

How did you hear of this opening? _____

When can you start? _____ Desired Wage € _____

Are you looking for full-time employment?   ❑ Yes   ❑ No

If no, what hours are you available? _____

Are you willing to work shifts?   ❑ Yes   ❑ No

If yes, give details _____

Education

      School   Year   Qualification

School _____   _____ _____

Other Training _____   _____ _____

In addition to your work history, are there other skills, qualifications, or experience that we should consider? _____

_____

46

Transition Year Employment History (Start with most recent employer)

Company Name _____

Address _____ Telephone _____

Date Started _____ Starting Wage _____ Starting Position _____

Date Ended _____ Ending Wage _____ Ending Position _____

Name of Supervisor _____ May we contact? ❑ Yes ❑ No

Responsibilities_____

_____

_____

_____

Company Name _____

Address _____ Telephone _____

Date Started _____ Starting Wage _____ Starting Position _____

Date Ended _____ Ending Wage _____ Ending Position _____

Name of Supervisor _____ May we contact? ❑ Yes ❑ No

Responsibilities_____

_____

_____

_____

Attach additional information if necessary.

I certify that the facts set forth in this application for employment are true and complete to the best of my knowledge. I understand that if I am employed, false statements on this application shall be considered sufficient cause for dismissal.

Signature_____ Date _____

47

House Number
Your Street
Town/City
County

Today's date

Person's Name
Position
Company Name
Address

Dear (person's name)

Ref: Job Title / Vacancy / Reference Number

The opening paragraph should state *why* you are writing ie applying for a position and when you saw it advertised.

Your middle paragraph should *stimulate interest* in you, make your *enthusiasm* and *interest* in the job very *obvious* and create a desire on the part of the reader to interview you. Give *details* of your *background* that will show why you should be considered, referring to general qualifications, work experience or interests related to the position.

In your closing paragraph *refer* to some part of your *CV* and say that further details will be supplied if requested.

Yours sincerely

Your Signature
Your Name

Using the template write a cover letter for your career investigation job:

Your C.V.

Your Name

Personal Details

D.O.B: _____   Phone: *Mobile   /   Landline*

Address: *Address line 1,   Address line 2,   Address line 3,   County*

Email: _____

Personal Statement

_____

_____

_____

Education

Dates   Name of School

Junior Cert.

SUBJECT	LEVEL	GRADE

Work Experience

Dates _____

Job Title: _____

Name & address of company: _____

Duties Included:

List the jobs you did using words like organised, completed, co-ordinated, was

responsible for, and other such phrases to show that you are someone who

achieves and is not a 'robot'. _____

_____

_____

Hobbies & Interests

Sport or interest: _____ *Give further details of medals won or other*

achievements _____

_____

References

1) *Your Principal (with address and phone number)* _____

_____

2) *A boss from one of your work experiences (with address and phone*

number) _____

UNIT 10

Preparing For Interviews

Phone Call To Employer – Script

Pair up with a classmate and write a conversation that you could have with an employer.

Sit back to back, record this conversation and play it back for your class.

You: _____

_____

Employer: _____

_____

You: _____

_____

Employer: _____

_____

You: _____

_____

Employer: _____

You: _____

_____

Employer: _____

_____

You: _____

_____

Employer: _____

You: _____

Phone Call To Employer - Rate Yourself

Give yourself and others a grade by ticking the appropriate box:

Group	1	2	3	4	5	6	7
A Grade							
B Grade							
C Grade							
D Grade							
E Grade							
F Grade							

Which conversation was the best and why?   Best pair _____

What was good about it?

List five things that *should* be done in advance of an interview:

1	
2	
3	
4	
5	

Review of Interviews

Write down five things she did <u>wrong.</u>

1	
2	
3	
4	
5	

Write down five things he did <u>right.</u>

1	
2	
3	
4	
5	

Mock Interviews

Pick one option:

Description	Choice
A student interviewing another student with the teacher providing a standard set of questions for the interviewer.	
Teachers or someone from the local community interviewing students.	
Scripted role plays with students taking turns to participate or observe.	

Perhaps make a video of these role plays.

Self-Evaluation Of Your Own Mock Interview

Area	5	4	3	2	1
Education, competence for the role					
Relevant experience					
Knowledge of the job specification					
Knowledge of the company & background research					
Your skills and attitude					
Enthusiasm					
How you present yourself					

Rate your own performance above. Then ask your teacher to score your performance also. Do your scores differ? If yes, discuss why.

What to do if you don't get the interview or the job?

1	
2	
3	
4	

55

Quiz Time

1. A good way to prepare for an interview is:
   a) Go out the night before with friends and relax   ☐
   b) To research the company and plan what to wear   ☐
   c) Eat a lot of garlic bread before going in   ☐
   d) To get someone I know to put in a good word for me   ☐

2. In a phone interview it's a good idea to:
   a) Lie on a bed and relax   ☐
   b) Get a headset, be standing, dress well and be in a quiet place   ☐
   c) Have a funny answer message on my phone   ☐
   d) Be out shopping when I am expecting the call   ☐

3. If you don't get the interview or job you should:
   a) Get angry and seek out revenge   ☐
   b) Whinge and cry about how unfair the world is   ☐
   c) Blame my parents for the terrible genes they gave me   ☐
   d) Call the company and politely enquire where I went wrong   ☐

4. What should you wear for an interview?
   a) What I like because "it is what's on the inside that counts"   ☐
   b) Conservative clothes in dark colours, a suit is a good idea.   ☐
   c) Get the jewels on and show them how classy I am   ☐
   d) Make sure they can see my tattoo, it cost me a lot of money   ☐

5. What do you need to bring to an interview?
   a) C.V., cover letter and references just in case they are requested   ☐
   b) Nothing, all the stuff they need is already with them   ☐
   c) My dog as pets can be great company when you're stressed   ☐
   d) My mother or father   ☐

Your Score out of 5 [ ]

UNIT 11

The Gap Year Option

What is a Gap Year?

What is <u>NOT</u> a Gap Year?

1	
2	
3	

Benefits of a Gap Year

1	
2	
3	
4	
5	
6	
7	

Profiles of potential Gap Year students

1	
2	
3	
4	
5	
6	

Cost

Tips for planning

1	
2	
3	

List the details of three Gap Year organisations:

Name	
Website	
Phone No.	
Name	
Website	
Phone No.	
Name	
Website	
Phone No.	

58

Quiz Time

1. A Gap Year is:
    a) A structured period of personal growth ☐
    b) Living at home and hanging out ☐
    c) Going to Europe or Southeast Asia to party ☐
    d) Working a non-career related job to save money for college ☐

2. Type of people that do well on a Gap Year:
    a) Very funny but lazy people ☐
    b) People that love home and don't like travel ☐
    c) People with initiative, curiosity and imagination ☐
    d) Those that love fashion and shopping ☐

3. What are the benefits of a Gap Year?
    a) Begin to travel and never return home, ever ☐
    b) Watching two box sets a week ☐
    c) Getting a great tan ☐
    d) Gap Year students have better results than traditional students ☐

4. What is a typical profile of a potential Gap Year student?
    a) A student on parole from prison ☐
    b) An academic student overwhelmed by the college search process ☐
    c) A teacher on a career break ☐
    d) A managing director of a major tech company ☐

5. How much money will a Gap Year cost?
    a) €10,000 ☐
    b) Free ☐
    c) You pay for it as you work and can leave when debt is paid ☐
    d) Ranges between €3,000-€7,000 ☐

| Your Score out of 5: | |

Answers: 1a, 2c, 3d, 4b, 5d

Unit 12

Apprenticeships

What is an apprentice?

The apprenticeships that interest me are:

1	
2	
3	

What happens in each phase?

Phase 1	Phase 2	Phase 3	Phase 4	Phase 5	Phase 6	Phase 7

The minimum age is: _____

The minimum entry requirements are:

Traditional	New Apprenticeship

The steps to applying are:

1	
2	
3	

How is it assessed? _____

What QQI Level would I be on as a qualified apprentice? _____

Is the qualification recognised outside Ireland?   *Circle*   Yes   No

Can you continue to study afterwards?   *Circle*   Yes   No

How much does it cost?

Criteria	Four Year Degree	Apprenticeship
CAO Points		
Training Costs		
Training Salary		
Qualified Weekly Pay		

Difference in becoming qualified: | € |

61

6TH YEAR

Unit 13

Stress Management

Part 1: What Is Stress?

___

Stress feelings:

1	
2	
3	
4	
5	
6	

My external stressors are:

___

My internal stressors are:

___

Negative stress effects:

___

Positive stress benefits:

___

My body responses to stress:

[ ]

Stages of stress:

1	
2	
3	

Symptoms of stress:

1	
2	
3	
4	

My physical symptoms:

[ ]

My mental symptoms:

[ ]

My behavioural symptoms:

[ ]

My emotional symptoms:

[ ]

Part 2: Self-Help - The ABC Strategy

A = Awareness

What causes me stress?

```
┌─────────────────────────────────────────────┐
│                                             │
│                                             │
│                                             │
└─────────────────────────────────────────────┘
```

How do I react?

```
┌─────────────────────────────────────────────┐
│                                             │
│                                             │
│                                             │
└─────────────────────────────────────────────┘
```

B = Balance

Is stress a negative influence in your life   **Yes** ☐   No ☐

C = Control

Five things I can do to help myself combat the negative effects of stress (Stress Management Techniques).

1	
2	
3	
4	
5	

Stress is normal

If you manage it well, stress can be very positive.

Quiz Time

1. **What is stress?**
   a) When we are pulled in two different directions ☐
   b) Not getting to read any social media for one whole day ☐
   c) A reaction to excessive pressures or demands ☐
   d) All of the above ☐

2. **What lifestyle choice contributes to stress?**
   a) Staying up at night on social media causing sleep deprivation ☐
   b) Exercising for half an hour a day ☐
   c) Eating a balanced diet ☐
   d) Meditating for twenty minutes a day ☐

3. **What is a mind trap?**
   a) A type of mind control apparatus developed by the government ☐
   b) The education system ☐
   c) A technique that a hypnotist uses ☐
   d) Having unrealistic expectations, all or nothing thinking ☐

4. **What are the stages of stress?**
   a) Ok, bad and Oh My God! ☐
   b) The Olympia, The Gate and The Abbey ☐
   c) Alarm response, adaption and exhaustion ☐
   d) Ignore, stay oblivious and denial ☐

5. **To combat stress, we must first:**
   a) Have a lot of money for psychotherapy ☐
   b) Be aware that you are stressed ☐
   c) Be in top physical condition ☐
   d) Have healthy relationships with all our family members ☐

6. **What is Reframing?**
   a) Moving a picture into a nicer frame ☐
   b) Setting up a different friend to take the blame ☐
   c) A way of dealing with the past and remembering differently ☐
   d) A technique to change the way you see things ☐

Your Score out of 6: ☐

Answers: 1d,2a,3d,4c,5b,6d

Do Not Photocopy Thank You

Unit 14

The National Framework Of Qualifications - NFQ

A system of ten levels that describes the Irish qualifications system.

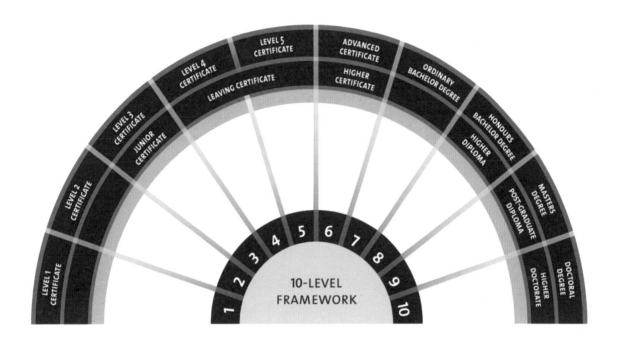

1.   Add a **cross** to the level you are at now.

2.   Tick the level you will be at after your Leaving Cert.

3.   Place an **arrow** at the level you will achieve after going to college, apprenticeship or university.

Quiz Time

1. Why was the NFQ developed?
   a) To confuse students about college ☐
   b) To make the education system more transparent ☐
   c) **N**annies **F**rom **Q**uebec needed to be organised ☐
   d) It was an opportunity to change all the qualification names ☐

2. How many levels are there on the NFQ?
   a) 22 ☐
   b) 5 ☐
   c) 100 ☐
   d) 10 ☐

3. Where else are NFQ qualifications recognised?
   a) Only recognised in Ireland ☐
   b) They are recognised worldwide ☐
   c) In a remote part of Outer Mongolia only ☐
   d) West Cork ☐

4. What Level would you be at if you did a Doctorate?
   a) Level 8 ☐
   b) Level 5 ☐
   c) Level 7 ☐
   d) Level 10 ☐

5. What do the letters NFQ mean?
   a) National Forum for Quotations ☐
   b) National Framework of Qualifications ☐
   c) Nannies From Quebec ☐
   d) Not For Quitters ☐

Your Score out of 5: [ ]

Do Not Photocopy Thank You

Unit 15

Studying Abroad

<u>UK & Northern Ireland</u>

Country	Amount of Universities/Colleges
England	
Scotland	
Wales	
Northern Ireland	
Total Number on UCAS System	

Amount of Universities/Colleges in Ireland _____

Approximately _____ Irish students accept places on courses in the UK each year.

I can apply to a max of _____ choices. One choice costs £_____. After that, 2 - 5 choices cost £_____ in total.

<u>Key Dates</u>

Description	Date
Website 'Apply' open to learners	
First day for receipt of applications	
Deadline for Medicine & Dentistry, Oxford or Cambridge	
Advisory application deadline (UK/EU)	
Last date to add 'Extra' choice	
Some art & design course applications	
Latest date for international applicants	

Do Not Photocopy Thank You

UCAS Application Sections

1	
2	
3	
4	
5	
6	

Personal Statement

1	
2	
3	
4	
5	

List some common errors found on personal statements:

1	
2	
3	
4	
5	
6	

Do Not Photocopy Thank You

"Track" Facility

1	
2	
3	
4	
5	

Decisions

Universities and colleges will make a decision based on:

1	
2	
3	
4	
5	
6	

What are the three types of decisions?

1	
2	
3	

Your Replies

What is a "Firm choice"?	What is an "Insurance choice"?

71

Confirmation Of Places

Exam results are published and sent to universities and colleges by UCAS. There are four possible outcomes:

1	2
3	4

Other Options

"Extra" is used when:

Europe

Some useful websites explaining all about studying in Europe:

USA

Some good websites explaining all about studying in the USA:

Do Not Photocopy Thank You

Quiz Time

1. How many Universities or Colleges are in the UK?
   a) 109 ☐
   b) 385 ☐
   c) 1208 ☐
   d) 38 ☐

2. Which country in the UK has no fees?
   a) Northern Ireland ☐
   b) England ☐
   c) Wales ☐
   d) Scotland ☐

3. What website would you use to apply to UK colleges?
   a) www.cao.ie ☐
   b) www.unicas.ie ☐
   c) www.ucas.com ☐
   d) www.sat.com ☐

4. Number of undergraduate programmes in Europe taught through English?
   a) 1200 ☐
   b) 7009 ☐
   c) 67 ☐
   d) None ☐

5. Where are the free fees in Europe?
   a) Austria ☐
   b) Netherlands ☐
   c) Germany ☐
   d) Scandinavian countries ☐

6. USA average college fees are:
   a) $25,000 ☐
   b) $12,000 ☐
   c) $5,000 ☐
   d) $500,000 ☐

Your Score out of 6: ☐

73

Unit 16

Central Applications Office - CAO

Points scale - fill in the blanks.

Higher Grade	Points	Ordinary Grade	Points
H1 90-100%		O1 90-100%	56
H2 80<90%	88	O2 80<90%	
H3 70<80%		O3 70<80%	37
H4 60<70%	66	O4 60<70%	
H5 50<60%		O5 50<60%	20
H6 40<50%	46	O6 40<50%	
H7 30<40%		O7 30<40%	0
H8 0<30%	0	O8	

Higher Level Subjects

_____ points are offered for grades of 30-39% for a "fail".

Higher Maths

A grade of 40 % in Higher Maths will get _____ bonus points.

Vital Course Information

What I think is vital information to find out about a course:

Getting The Information

What I think will be the best way of getting the information about courses:

R.T.F.M. stands for:

R	
T	
F	
M	

The white pages cover_____

The yellow pages cover _____

Choosing Your Courses

I can choose up to _____ honours degree / Level 8 courses. I can choose up to _____ higher certificate / ordinary degree / Level 6 & 7 courses. I _____ have to fill out all 10. I don't have to fill out _____. Each list is _____ of the other. I can be _____ choices from both lists. I can only choose _____ when/if offered.

Making Your Choice

I should choose in genuine _order of Preference_. My first choice is _the course I want the most_ to do most. I should ignore _____ _____. Go for what I want most. I need to keep at least "_one dead cert_" in my choices.

What I Need For Third Level:

C - College (Or Basic) Requirements: _4_ O6 in Leaving Certificate for Level 6 & 7 courses. Level 8 courses need a pass in _____ subjects with at least _____ at H5 & _____ at O6.

F – Faculty: The faculty (or course) _Requirements_ e.g. H5 in Irish for primary teaching, H5 in Maths for Engineering.

P – Points: Best _6_ subjects in _1_ sitting of the Leaving Certificate.

How The CAO Works

I get an offer when I satisfy all _____ Requirements, _____ Requirements & _____ Requirements. Some people don't accept offers, so I can get a higher up offer in round _2_ or _3_ .

CAO Application Number

I am now given _a CAO login password_ (sent instantly by email and text). I should keep this _safe_. I will need it to _login_ my account. I can _use change of mind_ free of charge until _____. After that _changes_ can be made from _may 1_ to _July 1_ .

Restricted Applications

Some _consider_ consider more then _1 entry requirement_ _____, _____, _____, _____ or _____. These are conducted around _march, April_. These courses _____ be added to my application after _____. They can be _____ or _____.

Confirmation

In ___may___ I will be sent a ___Statement___ of course choices. _____
all details _____. If there are no errors, I _____ need to do
___nothing___. _____ CAO of any errors by _____ them on the
form and _____ it back.

Change Of Mind

I will also be sent a _____ form in May. I can change
my mind _____ even if I have applied _____. The
_____ for changing my mind is _____.

Offers & Acceptance

Made _____ after Leaving Cert results. Made by _____ &
_____. I can _____ (Levels 6 & 7 &
Level 8). I can _____ one. I can accept _____ or by _____
_____ need to pay any _____. Start looking for my _____!

Available Places

In August, courses with places _____, or new courses are
_____ on the website www.cao.ie. I can apply for these provided I have
the _____ for them. I _____ have to have
made an application to CAO to avail of these. They can be worth checking out.

Deferring A Place

Deferring means that I _____ my place this year but
will do so next year. Some courses _____ be deferred, check beforehand.
Once the offer comes _____. I should
write IMMEDIATELY to _____.
_____ me know if the offer can be deferred.

Accepting A Deferred Course The Following Year

_____ the following year with _____ as my only choice. I will then get offered it in _____. If I put any _____ on the form, I will _____ my deferred place. I then _____ for places with all _____ applicants.

Important Information

If I have lived _____, see page _____ of Handbook. I may be _____ to apply _____ to some HEI's.

If exempt from _____ and/or _____ I must click the "Modify NUI Exemption Status" button & follow _____ to ensure I meet the entry requirements for NUI Colleges.

Important Dates

Date	Event
Nov _____	
Jan _____	
Feb _____	
May _____	
July _____	
Week After LC Results	
Early Sept	
As necessary	

Finally

Get lots of information.   Read the instructions.   Be on time.

Courses should be in my _____.

Include one "_____".

Do Not Photocopy Thank You

Quiz Time

1. When applying for courses it's best to:
   a) Put them in order of preference ☐
   b) Choose the ones with highest points first ☐
   c) Pick the ones your friends are going to ☐
   d) Choose the one that could earn you the most money ☐

2. What three requirements need to be satisfied before you are accepted to a course?
   a) Height, weight and age ☐
   b) Have done three subjects at honours level ☐
   c) Faculty, College and Points ☐
   d) Nationality, hair colour and a nice accent. ☐

3. The CAO number is:
   a) Issued to you by text or email after you pay on-line ☐
   b) Sent by post after the Leaving Cert. results come out ☐
   c) Is the same as your PPS Number ☐
   d) Made up by you when you apply ☐

4. If a course is restricted it means:
   a) There are less than ten places on the course ☐
   b) Only open to people in the Fine Gael Party ☐
   c) They can't be added to your application after February 1st ☐
   d) Only people from fee paying schools are allowed apply ☐

5. "Change of Mind" is a facility that allows you to:
   a) Change course choice anytime you like ☐
   b) Make course changes in May and June ☐
   c) Decide not to do the Leaving Cert and go on holiday instead ☐
   d) Change your politics ☐

6. **Offers & Acceptance:**
   a) As long as you have the points you can choose any course ☐
   b) You must write to the CAO in Sept to see if you were accepted ☐
   c) You will need to pay €50 fee to accept your course ☐
   d) If offered two courses you can only accept one ☐

7. If applying for "Available Places" in August:
   a) Most courses have available places and the points race is a myth ☐
   b) Available Places are advertised on Qualifax ☐
   c) Make sure you bring a tent, toilet roll and a phone charger ☐
   d) Apply via www.cao.ie, it is open to new and existing applicants ☐

Your Score out of 7:	

Do Not Photocopy Thank You

Unit 17

HEAR & DARE - <u>Higher Education Access Route - HEAR</u>

HEAR is not SUSI but if I apply for HEAR. I should also _____ to SUSI.

Why apply to Hear?

1	
2	

Write down the application criteria for HEAR:

1	
2	
3	
4	
5	
6	

How do I apply?

1	
2	
3	
4	

When you fill in your on-line HEAR application _____
_____ at the end.

Helpful tips:

1	
2	
3	
4	
5	
6	
7	
8	

Disability Access Route to Education - DARE

Who should apply?

1	
2	
3	

Do you think you might qualify to apply?   Yes ☐   No ☐

How do I apply?

1	
2	
3	
4	

Fill in the HEAR & DARE time sheet:

1st March	
1st April	
Late June	
July	
August	
Late August Early Sept	

I can apply to _____ HEAR & DARE

Documents I need:

1	
2	
3	
4	

Clinics in my area are:

Date _____   Place _____

81

Quiz Time

1. What is HEAR & DARE?
   a) An application process that makes access to education fairer for all ☐
   b) Two places that you can be in, one is hear and the other is dare ☐
   c) A pro-hunting organisation that promotes blood sports ☐
   d) It's a gameshow on TV where participants are dared to do things ☐

2. Are all 3rd level colleges involved?
   a) Yes, all PLC, Universities and Institutes of Technology ☐
   b) No, but full details are on www.accesscollege.ie ☐
   c) Private colleges only ☐
   d) No, only colleges in Dublin ☐

3. Are there reduced CAO Points on offer?
   a) Usually, but it cannot be guaranteed ☐
   b) Yes, a definite 50 points off every course ☐
   c) Each course has an agreed reduction in points ☐
   d) No, extra points are added to Level 6 courses ☐

4. How do I apply for HEAR or DARE?
   a) Write to each college you are applying to ☐
   b) Select the HEAR &/or DARE option on the CAO form ☐
   c) Tell your Guidance Counsellor ☐
   d) Ask at your local Post Office ☐

5. What supporting documents do I need to submit?
   a) None they can figure it out from your PPS number ☐
   b) Your school will take care of it for you ☐
   c) A check list of documents will be generated on the on-line form ☐
   d) Just send in your passport ☐

6. **What is the deadline for applications?**
   a) February 1st ☐
   b) August ☐
   c) Late June ☐
   d) March 1st ☐

7. How do you prove a disability?
   a) Get your doctor to phone the DARE helpline ☐
   b) Provide a report that is less than 3 years old ☐
   c) No need, they will believe you ☐
   d) You will need to attend an interview in the DARE office ☐

Your Score out of 7:

Answers: 1a,2b,3a,4b,5c,6d,7b.

Do Not Photocopy Thank You

Unit 18

Student Grants – SUSI (Student Universal Support Ireland)

SUSI can pay up to € _____ in college fees.

Maintenance Grant

If I live *less* than 45km from College SUSI can pay up to € _____

If I live *more* than 45km from College SUSI can pay up to € _____

I could get a _____ maintenance grant if our family income is below €_____

Grant types and rates are dependent on my _____

I can get 25%, _____%, _____% or 100% grants depending on financial circumstances.

The maintenance grant comes in _____ instalments.

Key Eligibility Criteria

1	
2	
3	
4	
5	

SUSI Key Dates

Event	Date
Applications Open	
Renewal Applications Close	
New Applications Close	

If I apply to SUSI, I _____ _____ the _____ option on my _____ so the CAO can inform SUSI of a college place offer. I can check out my grant eligibility at www.susi.ie.

Quiz Time

1. How many students applied to SUSI last year?
   a) 2,500 ☐
   b) 103,000 ☐
   c) 50,000 ☐
   d) 75,000 ☐

2. How much money is available to you for college registration fees?
   a) €3000 ☐
   b) €2000 ☐
   c) €500 ☐
   d) None, pay it your self ☐

3. What is a maintenance grant?
   a) A payment that helps you stay fit ☐
   b) A sum of money you need to pay your ex-husband or ex-wife ☐
   c) Money granted to you for living expenses in college ☐
   d) Money given to you when you apply ☐

4. How far away from college do you need to live to be given the non-adjacent grant?
   a) More than 45km ☐
   b) More than 100Km ☐
   c) Just don't live opposite the college you are attending ☐
   d) Only given to you if you go to college in the UK ☐

5. How do you apply for the grant?
   a) Write a letter to the government explaining your situation ☐
   b) Go www.susi.ie and apply from there. ☐
   c) It comes into your bank account automatically ☐
   d) Tick the SUSI option on the CAO form ☐

6. If you repeat a year in college can you apply for a SUSI grant?
   a) As long as you are in college you will get a grant ☐
   b) SUSI will feel sorry for you and increase the amount ☐
   c) You will be given no money if you repeat a year ☐
   d) Only half a grant will be offered ☐

Your Score out of 6	

Answers: 1b,2a,3c,4a,5d,6c

Unit 19

The Post Leaving Cert Option

Post Leaving Cert Courses are for:

1	
2	
3	
4	

They offer a great _____ of courses in your locality designed for

_____ you want to get into. An alternative _____ into university

or college. Often acts like a "_____" into college or university. PLC

graduates _____ go on to gain higher education and training awards too. Each

course has _____ minimum entry requirements. You will need to know them!

Higher Education Links Scheme To University and Institutes of Technology

University places can be _____ for Level 5 Certificate (NFQ Level 5) holders.

Offered in order of merit based on ranking. Currently, approximately _____%
of CAO applicants are Level 5 Certificate (NFQ Level 5) holders.

Always _____ with Institutes of Technology Admissions Office.

Institutes of Technology do not _____ between Leaving Certificate
and Level 5 Certificate (NFQ Level 5) holders.

Progression from Advanced Certificate (NFQ Level 6)

Learners can _____ into Year 2 of an appropriate course in an
Institute of Technology.

Nursing Applications

Only _____ places nationwide are reserved for nursing degrees. Applicants are

chosen by _____ selection for places. In all cases applicants must have

achieved at least 5 _____ because of the scarcity of nursing places.

_____ the Leaving Cert is an option.

Students With Additional Needs

Students are _____ to same supports they received in secondary

school.

Applications

If is student is genuinely interested in a PLC course or wishes to have a PLC course as a

back-up plan, then they need to apply as _____ as possible to get a place.

Cost

Great Value at 10% of the _____ of College or University!!

SUSI Grants

You can also receive a _____ grant from SUSI when doing a PLC Course.

Quiz Time

1. The fees for a PLC course are around:
   a) €2,500 ☐
   b) €3,000 ☐
   c) €300 ☐
   d) Free ☐

2. How many PLC courses are there in the country?
   a) 1,857 ☐
   b) 300 ☐
   c) 150 ☐
   d) 5,000 ☐

3. How do you apply for a PLC Course?
   a) Use the CAO form ☐
   b) Apply via the college's website ☐
   c) Turn up in Sept and tell the college what course you want to do ☐
   d) Tell your Guidance Counsellor to do it for you ☐

4. Can you go on to an IT / university after you graduate from a PLC?
   a) Yes, different courses can be linked to PLC courses ☐
   b) No, universities don't like PLC graduates ☐
   c) Yes, but you must do a doctorate degree first ☐
   d) After a PLC you are never allowed to study again ☐

5. Can you apply for a student grant?
   a) No, PLC courses are not funded by SUSI ☐
   b) Yes, but you can only claim for a maintenance grant ☐
   c) No, but the college pays you to attend lectures ☐
   d) Yes, full fees and maintenance grants are paid ☐

6. What percent of CAO applicants have a PLC Qualification?
   a) 8% ☐
   b) 7% ☐
   c) 2% ☐
   d) 15% ☐

Your Score out of 6:

Unit 20

Transition To College

List three things you are looking forward to at college:

1	
2	
3	

And three fears you might have about going to college:

1	
2	
3	

Features Of College

	Can you do this?
Independent Study: You have to study without the teacher directing your every move. There are not always notes to learn off, nor always "right answers", you have to support all your arguments with examples, quotes and references. **Hint:** Attend all lectures and classes, labs and tutorials. Ask for help if you are lost.	Yes ☐ No ☐ Maybe ☐

	Can you do this?
Higher Level Study: Courses are demanding and you will have to work. Read and write about Shakespeare plays on your own. Translate and improve your foreign language skills. Learn advanced maths calculations and formulas. Conduct scientific experiments. **Hint:** Personal reading and writing, exploring your chosen subject through the media and online.	Yes ☐ No ☐ Maybe ☐

	Can you do this?
Making deadlines, completing assignments: While you don't have homework you do have assignments, many of which count for assessment. Can you pace yourself to work on these assignments? **Hint:** Don't leave it to the last minute. Begin as soon as you get them. Don't let them accumulate. Keep working on them and revise and update regularly.	Yes ☐ No ☐ Maybe ☐

| Making Friends: Your existing friends are unlikely to end up doing your course, so you will have to make new ones. Even if some do go you'll still be expanding your circle of friends.

Hint: Get talking to someone at each class or lecture. Join clubs and societies. Consider everyone you meet as a potential friend, almost all are in the same boat.	Can you do this? Yes ☐ No ☐ Maybe ☐
Fitting in: You may be conscious of your accent, your lack of knowledge, your lack of money or your "oddness".

Hint: Colleges are full of odd bods and eccentrics and are very accepting of differences. Everybody is new and all find it hard to adjust. Be yourself, and if you accept others, they will accept you no matter how different you are. | Can you do this?

Yes ☐

No ☐

Maybe ☐ |
| Drinking and Partying: Colleges are notorious for these activities. It may sound strange, but can you handle these?

Hint: Never drink to the point of blacking out. Be aware of the dangers involved in heavy drinking and excessive partying. Never miss a lecture or class because of it and don't do it the night before your placements or exams. | Can you do this?

Yes ☐

No ☐

Maybe ☐ |

This is what it costs to go to college for the year:

Annual Cost of Living for Students	Living Away From Home	Living at Home	Living Away From Home in Dublin
Rent (National average) €400	3600	0	6000
Utilities	297	0	297
Food	1548	585	1800
Travel	1100	700	1100
Books	495	495	495
Clothes/Medical	400	400	400
Mobile	288	288	288
Social life/Misc	1188	1188	2000
Student Contribution Charge	3000	3000	3000
Totals	€11,916	€6,656	€15,380

Costs of College: College is expensive – living away from home, fees, books, materials & transport costs. Hint: Keep money for essential things, do not squander it; avail of student offers. If you can't afford it, do without it.	Can you do this? Yes ☐ No ☐ Maybe ☐

Are you ready?

No. of Yes		No. of No		No. of Maybe	

List three things you can do to be more prepared:

1) _____

2) _____

3) _____

Do you now feel you are really ready for college? Why?

Do Not Photocopy Thank You

Quiz Time

1. **What is a thesis?**
   a) A subject you need to do in first year of college ☐
   b) A common room where students can relax ☐
   c) A type of hat professors wear ☐
   d) A written piece of research usually submitted for the final year ☐

2. **What is a masters?**
   a) A degree you do after your first degree (Level 9 NFQ) ☐
   b) A collection of professors from each subject in the University ☐
   c) A golf tournament held in the USA each year ☐
   d) A type of cane used to punish students in the mid twentieth century ☐

3. **What is a semester?**
   a) A type of motor bike very popular in India ☐
   b) Your first week in university where you can join the societies ☐
   c) A week you are given off to do independent research ☐
   d) A college term, usually there are two a year ☐

4. **What does an "Omnibus Entry" to a course mean?**
   a) An omnibus is a bus that services a university (e.g. No.10 for UCD) ☐
   b) That entry is permitted only for students that have studied Latin ☐
   c) A degree with subject options that students can select to study ☐
   d) Anyone can sign up to these courses and do them ☐

5. **What is a tutorial?**
   a) Teaching in a small group ☐
   b) A smaller section of a course ☐
   c) An educational holiday abroad to a European city during college term ☐
   d) Just another name for a lecture ☐

6. **What is a postgraduate course?**
   a) Learning done by post (more recently called an e-learning course) ☐
   b) A course you can apply for after you graduate ☐
   c) A job in the university held for exceptional students ☐
   d) A course exclusively for students that want to teach ☐

7. **What are credits?**
   a) Campus currency often used with a student card ☐
   b) People you need to thank at your graduation ceremony ☐
   c) Marks that are accumulated to go towards your qualification ☐
   d) Cash back from your registration fees when you graduate ☐

Your Score out of 7: _____

Answers: 1d, 2a, 3d, 4c, 5a, 6b, 7c.

Do Not Photocopy Thank You

Unit 21

Exam Technique

Who has most to fear from exams: the student who knows everything or the one who knows nothing?

The answer surprisingly is the one who knows everything, because they have to modify what they know into answering several questions in a few hours. Their problem is knowing when to stop and how to deal with the frustration of not being able to put all they know on the paper.

As for those who know nothing their problem is being creative in spinning the little knowledge they have into a possible answer. Don't try and do this!

- So the great day comes and you **find your spot** in the exam hall.

- Make sure you _____ you need pens, pencils and rulers etc. and do heed the classic advice of bringing a second pen!

- _____ completely in your seat. Let your hands hang, breathe deeply, close your eyes and say to yourself: *For the next few hours I will bring all my attention, ability & knowledge to this exam. I will have access to all the things I learned and everything I ever heard or read.*
I will be brilliant.

- _____.

  Make sure there are no surprises or major changes to cope with.

  "For the next few hours I will bring all my attention, ability & knowledge to this exam. I will have access to all the things I learned and everything I ever heard or read.

  I will be brilliant."

- _____ you will answer.

- _____
_____ in headings or mind maps or spider diagrams. (This way, as you work on one question you will also be subconsciously working on the rest).

- Start with your _____ question but don't fall into the trap of writing too much on it.

- _____ strictly.

- Leave _____ on the paper at the end of the question for things you might add in on the final read through.

- When the time allocated to that question is up, _stop_ even if you are not finished. Move on to the **next question** and again, time yourself _____ on this.

92

- If you _____ of something you can add to a further question as you are doing another, make a _____ on the scrap paper where you sketched out your answer.

- Leave yourself _____ at the end to _____, particularly check for misspellings caused by writing so fast. Add in any extra points at the end.

- If you have to re-start a question **do not obliterate it.** Draw an X through it and re-start. The examiners must correct every question on the paper and give you marks for the best version so _____ answers.

- If you have more time, _____. All questions have to be corrected and marks given to the best ones. So, if you have the time you can answer more.

- For essay type answers, have an _____, _____ well developed and well-argued _____ (supported by quotes and references) and a _____.

- Give your essays a _____; so turn the question into a **statement**: "The indecision of Hamlet" or "Nature imagery in Seamus Heaney"

- For Maths/Science type questions make sure you **show the workings** of any equation or problem. _____ are given for _____ step in the _____ so make sure the corrector can see every step you make.

- If certain questions are **ambiguous or obscure** or require information not on the course, _____ _____. You can state at the start of your answer that you are taking this interpretation of the question and answering it based on that. If such an issue arises the correctors will have to make allowances for it to be fair to all students.

- Make sure your _____, spare paper, different section or whatever you have to give back.

- _____ and ignore any "friends" who leave or invite you to go also.

- Keep the _____ _____.on the exams to a _____. Don't be put off by other approaches to the answers or their interpretation of the questions.

- Get ready to _____.in the next exam!

Very Important Point:

Do not change your CAO choices based on how you thought you did in the exams. Change your mind by all means, but do not let how you *thought* you did in the exams be a deciding factor in your choices.

Quiz Time

1. You should prepare answers for all your questions:
   a) Before you start writing the answers to any ☐
   b) As you go along in the exam ☐
   c) After you have done the first question ☐
   d) Once you have finished ☐

2. Why should you re-read your answers at the end?
   a) To see if you left anything out ☐
   b) To check your spelling from writing so fast ☐
   c) To add in any extra points you've thought of ☐
   d) All of the above ☐

3. If you have to restart a question you should:
   a) Obliterate your answer so it cannot be read ☐
   b) Cross it out but leave it legible ☐
   c) Ask for new paper and a new answer sheet ☐
   d) Just forget about that question ☐

4. For essay type questions you should:
   a) Answer with bullet points ☐
   b) Have well developed arguments supported by examples, quotes & evidence ☐
   c) Draw a picture ☐
   d) Give single word answers ☐

5. For maths and problem type questions you should:
   a) Show all your workings and calculations ☐
   b) Just put down the answer ☐
   c) Write a paragraph on your teacher ☐
   d) Do a freehand sketch with shading and tones ☐

6. If you have spare time at the end of an exam you should:
   a) Go out for a smoke ☐
   b) Do a sketch of the exam hall on your paper ☐
   c) Answer some more questions so they take the best ones ☐
   d) Take out your notes and start studying for the next exam ☐

Your Score out of 6:

Answers: 1a,2d,3b,4b,5a,6c

94

Unit 22

Future Skills

Write down five professions that catch your eye:

1	
2	
3	
4	
5	

Are you taking any steps to be able to access a career in some of the jobs above?

Yes ☐   No ☐

Explain

Quiz Time

1. When considering future career demands you should:
   a) Do everything possible to get into this area ☐
   b) Be aware of future trends but if it's not for you, that's ok ☐
   c) Not consider it, focus on yourself only ☐
   d) Doesn't matter, global warming will destroy everything ☐

2. The future will be a good place for:
   a) Most areas of engineering ☐
   b) Insurance underwriters ☐
   c) Travel Agents ☐
   d) Florists ☐

3. The future will also be a good place for:
   a) Typewriter repair people ☐
   b) Moulding machine operators ☐
   c) Woodworking machine operators ☐
   d) Anyone who is good at coding, software and analytics ☐

4. Why has the job of 'care worker' got a good future?
   a) Life expectancy is up and elderly people will need care ☐
   b) People on their phones all day will need help ☐
   c) The superbugs are coming ☐
   d) Robots are not sophisticated enough yet ☐

5. Having a second or third language is important because:
   a) You will order great food when on holidays abroad ☐
   b) You become more attractive to the opposite sex ☐
   c) Globalisation has created opportunities for the multi-lingual ☐
   d) You can read twice as many novels ☐

6. **The job of a Quantity Surveyor is:**
   a) To make sure a country has enough food to feed the population ☐
   b) To assess an architect's drawings and decide costs and time ☐
   c) To survey people on the street and publish polls ☐
   d) To get the quantities of ingredients right in food manufacturing ☐

Your Score out of 6:

Answers: 1b,2a,3d,4a,5c,6b

Unit 23

Not Going To College?

If you cannot go or don't want to go to college tick your preferred option(s) for next year

Options	Tick
Apprenticeship	
Army	
Garda	
Volunteer or Gap Year	
Get An Entry Level Job	
Teaching English as a Foreign Language	
Entrepreneurship	
(Other)	

Are you taking steps to be able to access a career in the option(s) you selected?

Yes ☐   No ☐

Explain:

Do Not Photocopy Thank You

Unit 24

Student Accommodation

The best port of call when hunting for a place to live is the _____.

Useful Websites

Digs is living with a _____ _____. Breakfast and evening meals are included from Monday to Friday.

Self-Catering/House Share is sharing a house or an apartment with _____ _____. Landlords are obliged to provide you with a rent book, written contract or lease.

On-Campus Student Accommodation is _____ by the _____ and is usually on or near campus.

Homestay.com offer _____ _____ affordable accommodation in _____ homes while you try to find long term accommodation.

Airbnb offer short term affordable accommodation while you _____ to find _____ _____ accommodation.

thehomeshare.ie links students interested in sharing a home with an _____ person. They might need a _____ with light _____ and some _____. Student benefits from _____ rent.

Of the different types of accommodation which would interest you the most and why?

Nine top tips for student accommodation

1	
2	
3	
4	
5	
6	
7	
8	
9	

Do Not Photocopy Thank You

Quiz Time

1. Where is the best place to start hunting for accommodation?
   a) The notices board in the local supermarket ☐
   b) On-line ☐
   c) Students' Union ☐
   d) Newspapers ☐

2. Which is a type of student accommodation?
   a) Digs ☐
   b) Self-Catering / House Share ☐
   c) On Campus student accommodation ☐
   d) All of the above ☐

3. Which is an emerging student accommodation option to keep in mind?
   a) Homestay.ie ☐
   b) Airbnb ☐
   c) Thehomeshare.ie ☐
   d) All of the above ☐

4. What does RTB stand for?
   a) Royal Tractor Brigade ☐
   b) Rent Together Board ☐
   c) Regional Tenants' Board ☐
   d) Residential Tenancies Board ☐

5. What is the RTB's main role?
   a) Prosecuting tenants for bad behaviour ☐
   b) Helping landlords get the best rent possible ☐
   c) Resolving disputes between landlords and tenants ☐
   d) All of the above ☐

6. Should you research your accommodation options?
   a) Yes, you should try and get the best available ☐
   b) No, there is an accommodation shortage so take what you are given ☐

Your Score out of 6: [   ]

Answers: 1c,2d,3d,4d,5c,6a

100

Unit 25

Scholarships & Bursaries

Which scholarships / bursaries from the Department of Education & Skills do you have a chance of being awarded?

Scholarship/ Bursary Name	Number Awarded	Value €	Application Needed?	Deis Schools?	Medical Card?	Am I eligible?

Which 3rd level college do you have the best chance of getting into?_____

What scholarship in this college is the most suitable to you? _____

Scholarship / Bursary name: _____

What category is it in? *(Tick box)*

Academic ☐   Sport ☐   Performing Arts ☐   Other _____ ☐

Value of Scholarship/Bursary is _____

Extra benefits if any are:

Free gym ☐   Free or subsidised accommodation ☐   Decreased CAO points ☐

Free coaching ☐   Other _____ ☐

Opening date ___/___/_____ and closing date for application ___/___/_____.

Are there interviews?   Yes ☐ No ☐   Dates if any ___/___/_____.

How do I apply? _____

_____

_____

Do Not Photocopy Thank You

Quiz Time

1. **What are scholarships?**
    a) A boat with students on board ☐
    b) An intensive study session that is never ending ☐
    c) Financial help or otherwise to encourage students with potential ☐
    d) An elaborate scam ☐

2. **Do you need to go to a Deis school to get a scholarship?**
    a) Yes, you also need a medical card ☐
    b) No, there are hundreds of scholarships for non-Deis schools ☐
    c) The All Ireland Scholarship is the only non-Deis award ☐
    d) No, but your family income needs to be below €25,000 ☐

3. **Are all scholarships based on academic results?**
    a) Yes, CAO points are the be all and end all ☐
    b) No, sports scholarships are the only other kind ☐
    c) No, only musicians need apply ☐
    d) No, Scholarships are there to promote potential in multiple areas ☐

4. **Can you get reduced CAO points on some scholarships?**
    a) Some scholarships let you in even if you fail the Leaving Cert ☐
    b) Points can be reduced to acknowledge exceptional achievements ☐
    c) CAO would never let this happen ☐
    d) Only if you are related to someone in the government ☐

5. **Do all scholarships need you to fill out an application form?**
    a) No, some will get your details from Dept of Education ☐
    b) Always, and it must be written by hand ☐
    c) Online applications are compulsory ☐
    d) No, some just call you for an interview ☐

6. **Do all scholarships have the same application closing date?**
    a) Yes, it is on April 1st each year ☐
    b) No, all have their own application procedures and closing dates ☐

Your Score out of 6:

Answers: 1c,2b,3d,4b,5a,6b

Unit 26

Checklist - Before You Leave School

	Have You...	Yes	No	*N/A
1	Applied to 10 CAO courses (Level 6, 7 or 8)?			
2	Applied to 5 or more PLC college courses?			
3	Understood all subjects in all applied for courses?			
4	Applied for jobs?			
5	Applied for apprenticeships?			
6	Are you aware of / applied for scholarships?			
7	A good C.V. and Cover Letter prepared?			
8	Applied for a SUSI grant?			
9	Applied to HEAR and / or DARE			
10	Made a plan for a Gap year if taking one?			
11	Considered if you are ready to leave school?			

*N/A = Not Applicable

If the answer is no to any of the above who do you need to talk to?

1	Guidance Counsellor	
2	Parent	
3	Principal	
4	Teacher	
5	Other	